1870s

The first bottle-making machines are built, making it possible to manufacture bottles in large numbers very quickly.

1608

Glassmaking begins in America, and glass windows become more common in Europe, even among poor people.

1959

The float glass process is introduced in Britain by Alastair Pilkington, enabling glassmakers to manufacture very smooth, flat glass more cheaply.

1674

Lead glass is invented in Britain by George Ravenscroft. Adding lead to glass improved its appearance and made it easier for glassmakers to melt and work with.

2000

Self-cleaning glass is invented in Britain. A thin chemical coating on the glass helps to break down dirt so that rain can wash it away.

1887

German chemist Otto Schott invents borosilicate glass, a type of glass that can withstand sudden temperature changes. It is used to make ovenproof glass bakeware.

What Is Glass?

Glass is a solid material. It is made of particles called atoms. The atoms in most solid materials are linked together in a neat pattern that repeats itself again and again. If you could see the atoms in a grain of sand, you would see them lined up in identical groups forming this regular, repeating pattern. Glass is made from sand, but the atoms in glass are linked together differently from sand.

Glass is made by heating sand until it melts. When sand melts, the links between some of its atoms break and so the atoms are able to move around. When the liquid sand cools down and begins to set hard, the atoms form new links with each other. Instead of the neat, regular crystal structure of sand, the atoms in glass are linked together in a messy, random way.

Author:

Ian Graham earned a degree in applied physics at City University, London. He then earned a graduate diploma in journalism. Since becoming a freelance author and journalist, he has written more than 250 children's nonfiction books.

Artist:

Mark Bergin was born in Hastings, England, in 1961. He studied at Eastbourne College of Art and specializes in historical reconstructions, aviation, and maritime subjects. He lives in Bexhill-on-Sea, England, with his wife and children.

Series creator:

David Salariya was born in Dundee, Scotland. He has illustrated a wide range of books and has created and designed many new series for publishers in the UK and overseas. David established The Salariya Book Company in 1989. He lives in Brighton, England, with his wife, illustrator Shirley Willis, and their son, Jonathan.

Editor: **Jacqueline Ford**

Editorial Assistant: **Mark Williams**

PAPER FROM
SUSTAINABLE
FORESTS

Published in Great Britain in 2017 by
The Salariya Book Company Ltd
25 Marlborough Place, Brighton BN1 1UB

ISBN-13: 978-0-531-22460-1 (lib. bdg.) 978-0-531-22489-2 (pbk.)

All rights reserved.
Published in 2017 in the United States
by Franklin Watts
An imprint of Scholastic Inc.

A CIP catalog record for this book is available
from the Library of Congress.

Printed and bound in China.
Printed on paper from sustainable sources.
1 2 3 4 5 6 7 8 9 10 R 27 26 25 24 23 22 21 20 19 18 17

JNF
661.1
GRAHAM

You Wouldn't Want to Live Without™
Glass!

Written by
Ian Graham

Illustrated by
Mark Bergin

Series created by
David Salariya

Franklin Watts®
An Imprint of Scholastic Inc.

Contents

Introduction

You use glass from morning till night every day, from the mirror you look in when you wash your face in the morning to the lightbulbs that brighten your home after dark. All sorts of foods and drinks are stored in glass bottles and jars, and many of your electronic gadgets have glass screens. Cameras and binoculars have lenses made of glass. The signals that carry your phone calls and texts—and Web sites when you're online—make part of their journey along glass communications cables. Every home, school, and workplace has glass windows. Can you imagine what your world and your life would be like if there were no glass? Buildings would have no windows. There would be no lenses for cameras or microscopes. There would probably be no televisions or computers. You really wouldn't want to live without glass.

THE VARIETY OF THINGS we use every day that depends on glass is astonishing. What do you think it would be like if all of these things were taken away from you?

What If There Were No Glass?

If people had never discovered how to make glass, many of the things you use would be different, and some might never have been invented at all. For example, polished metal might make a good mirror…until it gets scratched and dented. Nowadays, we could use clear plastic to replace glass, but if glass windows, screens, and bottles had never existed, would anyone have thought of the idea of inventing clear plastic?

LOOK AROUND YOU and see how many things you can spot that have glass parts. Are you wearing a watch or about to grab a glass of water? Is it time for your favorite show on TV? Glass is just about everywhere!

You Can Do It!

If there were no glass for mirrors, what else could you make a mirror from? Try kitchen foil, polished metal, and anything else you can think of. Do any of them work?

DARK CITIES. Cities all over the world are flooded with light at night. It shines out through glass windows and from glass streetlights. Storefronts are lit up by neon signs, too. Without glass for windows, lights, and glowing signs, our cities would be much darker places.

TRAFFIC CHAOS? Traffic at busy intersections is often controlled by colored light signals. They keep the traffic moving and stop the intersection from being blocked. If there were no glass, traffic lights might never have been invented and traffic jams, or gridlock, might be a lot more common today.

Nature's Glass

All the glass you see and use every day is manufactured. It was made by someone or by a machine. It is the size, shape, and color it is because it was designed and made like that. But even if people had never discovered how to make glass, we would still know about glass because it is also made by nature. In fact, nature has been making glass on Earth for billions of years. Any event in nature that produces enough heat to melt rock or sand is capable of making glass. Natural glass is produced by volcanoes, by lightning, and when large meteorites hit the ground. Meteorites are chunks of rock from space that survive their fiery journey down through Earth's atmosphere and land on the ground.

What's this?

It's volcanic glass.

VOLCANIC GLASS. When lava (hot liquid rock) from a volcano cools slowly, it becomes rock. But if it cools quickly, there is not enough time for the microscopic crystals that form rock to grow. Instead of rock, the result is volcanic glass. One of the best-known types of volcanic glass is called obsidian. It's hard and brittle, and usually black.

LIGHTNING GLASS.
When lightning strikes the ground, it instantly heats the spot to about 4,500 degrees Fahrenheit (2,500 degrees Celsius). That's hot enough to melt sand and change it to glass. As a lightning bolt travels down into the ground, it forms long, branching tubes of glass up to 17 feet (5 meters) long. These antler-like pieces of glass created by lightning are called fulgurites.

How It Works

Natural glass is rarely clear like a window, because it often includes small minerals that give it color, has a rough, uneven surface, lots of tiny cracks, and partly melted rock or sand sticking to it.

MYSTERY MATERIAL.
Thousands of years ago, our distant ancestors found pieces of natural glass. It must have seemed magical to them, quite unlike anything else in nature.

FROZEN SPLASHES. When a big meteorite hits Earth, it melts the rock at the spot where it lands. The liquid rock flies up into the air. The splashes cool down quickly, forming blobs of glass called tektites.

Before We Made Glass

Imagine if you lived in Europe about 500 years ago. You probably wouldn't own anything made of glass unless you were very wealthy. The windows in your home wouldn't have any glass in them. You wouldn't have any drinking cups made of glass. Instead you would drink from pottery cups, or—if you're lucky—goblets made of gold, silver, or a cheaper metal called pewter. You probably wouldn't even know what you look like, because you wouldn't own a glass mirror. You would have to get by without these things or use other materials instead of glass.

Who's that?

IF YOU HAD LIVED hundreds of years ago and you didn't have a mirror, the only time you might see your reflection would be when you spotted it in a pool of water. It might have been quite a surprise to see what you looked like!

As a person living in Europe in the Middle Ages, you'll want to bundle up during the winter. Since glass windows haven't been invented yet, it can be pretty drafty indoors!

HORN AND HIDE. Until about 400 years ago, the windows in many people's homes were either open to the weather or covered with animal hide or pieces of animal horn. The horn was so thin that it let some light through. Horn was much cheaper than glass, which was heavily taxed in some countries.

17th-century candle lantern with sheets of mica

MICA. Thin sheets of a material called mica were used instead of glass in some windows and lanterns. Mica is a naturally occurring mineral that can be split into very thin sheets. It was used, like animal horn, as a cheaper alternative to glass. It is also known as Muscovy glass.

BEFORE GLASS BOTTLES became widely available, bottles and other containers were made of clay pottery, metal, or even leather. When clay bottles broke, they were thrown away. They were so common that archeologists often find them buried in the ground.

A New Material

People have been using glass for thousands of years. At first, it was glass they found in nature. They used it to make blades. The ancient Aztec people of Mexico made cutting tools and weapons from natural glass. They also made glass jewelry. About 5,500 years ago, people in Mesopotamia and Egypt discovered how to make glass. They made glassy glazes for their pottery and then small glass objects such as beads. Larger items came later as their skills improved. If they had not learned how to make glass, we might not have the glass things that are so useful to us today.

AN ANCIENT AZTEC SWORD called a macuahuitl is a fearsome weapon. It was used right up to the sixteenth century. A macuahuitl was made by setting slivers of black obsidian glass along the edges of a wooden sword. The result was a weapon up to 4 feet (1.2 m) long and 3 inches (8 centimeters) across, weighing a hefty 6.6 pounds (3 kilograms). It was even sharper than a modern steel razor blade.

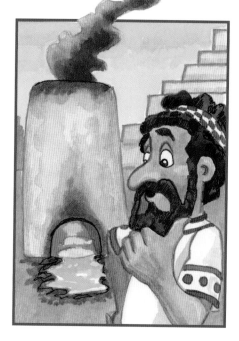

THE SECRET OF GLASSMAKING was probably discovered by accident. Perhaps some sand melted in a metalworking furnace and changed into glass. Maybe sand stuck to wet clay in a pottery kiln and formed a glassy glaze. It must have happened many times before anyone noticed, and many more times before someone thought of making glass deliberately by melting sand in a furnace.

THE ANCIENT EGYPTIANS made a glassy substance called faience. They made it by grinding up sand with other materials to produce a crunchy, claylike material. They then molded this into the shape of jewelry or small figures, and heated it in a furnace. The mixture partly melted and hardened, forming a glassy surface.

THE ANCIENT ROMANS were expert glassmakers. About 2,000 years ago, they were making all sorts of glass cups, bowls, and bottles. And they took their glassware with them all over the vast Roman Empire.

WHEN ARCHEOLOGISTS dig among ancient buildings or graves, they often find glass beads. They were worn as jewelry and traded for other items and services. They can help archeologists to date a site. Finding the same type of beads in different places can also help to show which settlements were trading with each other.

13

Making Glass

People make glass in a way that is very similar to how nature does it. They heat sand until it melts. Other substances are often added to help the sand melt and to color the glass. Adding small amounts of iron or chromium produces green glass. Cobalt and copper turn glass blue. Gold produces a red color. Glass used to be colored yellow by using radioactive uranium, until the dangers of uranium were discovered.

Once glass is made, it has to be shaped. Glass bottles, bowls, and other items can be made one at a time by skilled people, or they can be made more quickly in large numbers by using special machines.

A GLASSBLOWER makes hollow items by blowing air through a pipe into a blob of molten glass on the end of the pipe. The glass, at a temperature of just over 1,800°F (1,000°C), looks like soft toffee and blows up like a balloon.

Furnace

Former

Flux

Stabilizer

FOLLOW THE RECIPE. Glass is made of three basic materials—a former, a flux, and a stabilizer. The most common type of glass is called soda-lime glass. The former, or main substance, is silica (sand). The flux, usually sodium oxide from soda, lowers the sand's melting temperature. The stabilizer, usually calcium oxide from limestone, stops the glass from dissolving or crumbling after it cools and hardens.

THE MACHINES THAT MAKE GLASS BOTTLES use a process called blow molding. They lower a tube of glowing glass, called a gob, into a metal mold. The mold closes around the glass. Then air is blown in to inflate the glass and press it against the walls of the mold. This makes the glass take the shape of the mold. Finally, the mold opens and a glowing-hot glass bottle emerges.

Clearly Useful

The most useful property of glass is its transparency—its ability to let light pass through. It lets you see what kind of solid or liquid—and how much—is inside bottles and jars. And this transparency allows light out of lightbulbs. The glass bulb also keeps air out. Without glass bulbs, electric lights would burn out in seconds. If there were no glass, we might have to go back to using candles and gas lamps for lighting. And of course TV sets, computers, cell phones, wristwatches, and other electronic gadgets would be useless without their glass screens.

BULLS-EYE WINDOWS.
In the 1300s, French glassmakers invented a way to make glass for windows by spinning molten glass to make a flat disc. The middle was thicker than the edges. It was known as bulls-eye glass, or crown glass.

Which one's the sugar?

WITHOUT GLASS, you'd always have to open storage jars to find out what's inside.

Greenhouses work by letting sunlight pass through their glass roof and walls to warm everything inside. Then the glass traps the warm air inside so that it can't be blown away.

THE CYLINDER METHOD.

By the 1800s, windows were flatter than the old bulls-eye panes, because they were being made in a new way. They started as a long tube of glass, like a long party balloon, and then the glass was blown outward. While the glass was still hot and soft, the ends were cut off and the cylinder was slit from end to end. The slit cylinder was then opened out to make a flat sheet.

FLOATING FLAT. Modern window glass is very flat because of the way it is made. Hot glass is laid on the surface of molten tin. As the glass cools, it forms a perfectly flat sheet called float glass.

LABORATORY GLASS. The test tubes and flasks used in science laboratories are made of glass so that scientists can see what is happening to the chemicals inside them. Also, glass doesn't react with chemicals and change them in unwanted ways.

17

Making It Safe

Imagine a train or a car with no glass in its windows. Would you like to go for a trip in it on a cold day or when it's raining? Glass windows make trains, cars, and other vehicles weatherproof. In the past, vehicle windows were made of ordinary glass, but this proved to be dangerous. If a window broke it sent razor-sharp pieces of glass flying everywhere, so safer types of glass were invented. They still sometimes break, but they break in a safer way. Without them, traveling would be more dangerous.

A CAR WITHOUT GLASS would not be much fun to travel in. Luckily, glass was invented before cars. Today, car windows are made of two different types of safety glass—laminated glass and tempered glass. Tempered glass is toughened, or tempered, by treating it with heat or chemicals.

CRUMBS! When tempered glass breaks, it shatters into thousands of small glass crumbs. The rounded crumbs are less likely to cause injuries than the sharp splinters produced by ordinary glass. Tempered glass is used for a car's side windows and rear windows.

Top Tip

Newspaper is very good for cleaning glass. Some people think the ink on the paper polishes the glass. Others think it works because the paper is very absorbent. What do you think?

A GLASS SANDWICH. A car's windshield is made of laminated glass. It's a sandwich of sheets of glass with plastic between them. Laminated glass is used in other places, too, where the glass must stay together even when it breaks, such as in skyscraper windows.

BULLETPROOF. A window made of several layers of thick glass and plastic up to about 3.5 inches (9 cm) thick can stop a bullet. This type of bulletproof glass is used in places like banks, armored cars, and military vehicles.

STICKING TOGETHER. If a laminated windshield gets broken by a stone kicked up from the road, the glass might crack, but the plastic layer holds the pieces together and stops them from flying out and causing injuries.

Reflectors

The smooth, flat surface of a sheet of manufactured glass is very good at reflecting light. The reflection is brighter and clearer if the glass is coated with a thin film of shiny metal, forming a mirror. But mirrors do a lot more than let you check out your appearance. Without mirrors, we would know a lot less about the rest of the universe.

Astronomical telescopes use curved mirrors to focus light from distant stars and galaxies. The amazing photographs taken by the Hubble Space Telescope were made possible by the mirrors inside it. There are even mirrors on the moon. They were placed there by astronauts. Scientists use them to calculate the precise distance between Earth and the moon. Glass mirrors make driving safer, too.

THE HUBBLE SPACE TELESCOPE gathers light from distant parts of the universe. The light falls on a large primary mirror. It bounces onto a small secondary mirror and then into cameras and other instruments.

DRIVERS OFTEN NEED to know what's happening behind them. They do it by glancing in their rearview mirror. If there were no glass mirrors, drivers might have to take their eyes off the road and turn around, risking an accident.

A REFLECTION in a mirror is accurate and lifelike only if the mirror is flat. Amusement park fun houses make use of this. Their distorting mirrors are curved and wavy. They make reflections of people look very odd. Some parts are bigger and others are smaller.

Secondary mirror

Solar panel

Primary mirror

Camera

You Can Do It!

You can see the effect of a distorting mirror by looking at your reflection on the back of a spoon. Then turn the spoon over and see how different your reflection is on the other side.

THE GLASS STUDS that help define roads at night work by reflecting light from a vehicle's headlights. They're called cat's eyes, because the inventor got the idea for them when he saw a real cat's eyes shining brightly in his car headlights one night.

A CURVED MIRROR can concentrate sunlight and produce very high temperatures. In 2013, the curved glass wall of a new building in London focused sunlight onto the street below. A car parked there partially melted! The building has a sunshade now.

Light Benders

Light slows down a little as it travels through glass. This has a strange effect on the light. As it hits the glass and slows down, it changes direction. It's an effect called refraction and it can be very useful. A piece of glass shaped in a special way can bend light rays together or spread them apart. A piece of glass that does this is called a lens. Bending light rays like this can make things look bigger or smaller, closer or farther away. Because of this simple property of glass, we know more about everything from microscopic germs to vast galaxies of stars.

ONE OF THE FIRST THINGS astronomers used telescopes for was to look at the moon. They were amazed to see towering mountains, deep valleys, craters of all sizes, and vast flat plains in wonderful close-up detail. Astronomers still use telescopes to study the moon today.

BEFORE GLASS LENSES became common, very few people had eyeglasses. Some of the monks who wrote manuscripts and read books were among the few to own a pair. The lenses were set in a frame made from bone, metal, or leather that was balanced on the nose. Everyone else had to manage without glasses, no matter how poor their vision was.

You Can Do It!

You can see how glass bends light by putting a straw in a glass of water. The straw looks broken at the water's surface, because the light rays bend as they leave the glass of water.

SIR ISAAC NEWTON proved that sunlight contains light of all colors. He passed light through a glass wedge called a prism. The prism split the light into a rainbow of colors.

MICROSCOPES USE LENSES to magnify tiny things that are normally too small to be seen. The first microscopes in the 1590s revealed a hidden world of tiny organisms. Many of the organisms that cause diseases were discovered by scientists using microscopes.

Building With Glass

Mmmmm, dinner...

You might think that glass is a very weak and fragile material. Windows and glass vases break easily, but glass in a different form is strong enough to use as a building material. And glass blocks are sturdy enough to be used for building walls. The front wall of a giant public aquarium is often made of extremely strong glass. Glass has other properties that are useful to the construction industry. In the form of glass wool, it traps air inside it, and air is a good insulator. Double-glazed windows use air as an insulator, too. Air trapped inside them reduces the amount of heat that passes through. Without glass wool insulation and double glazing, buildings would be colder in winter and hotter in summer.

THE GLASS WALL that forms the front of the world's biggest public aquariums can be up to 30 inches (75 cm) thick. The glass has to be that thick to hold back the enormous weight of water behind it.

LARGE GLASS BLOCKS can be used like bricks to build walls and partitions inside buildings. They can be used outside in gardens, too. A glass-block wall can screen off a private space while letting light through.

LIGHT PIPES were recently invented to help guide sunlight into buildings. The inside of a light pipe is coated with a reflective material. Light normally travels only in straight lines, but light pipes can make light turn corners.

KEEPING WARM. Insulating roofs with glass wool helps keep buildings warm, like putting a warm hat on the building. The wool is in the form of thick mats that are unrolled in the building's roof space to stop precious heat from escaping. Walls are often insulated with glass wool as well.

FIBERGLASS. Embedding glass fibers in plastic produces a strong and light material called glass reinforced plastic (GRP), or fiberglass. Glass fibers are sprayed into a mold and soaked with liquid plastic, which then hardens. Some boats and car bodies are made from fiberglass.

Glass Art

Glass isn't used only to make practical everyday things like windows and television screens. It is also used by artists to make beautiful objects. Some artists specialize in making decorative glass vases, lampshades, jewelry, and other items. Some of the biggest and most visually stunning works of art ever produced are made of glass. These include the stained-glass windows of the world's most famous churches and cathedrals. Without glass, there would be none of this wonderful art for us to enjoy.

STAINED-GLASS WINDOWS in churches were designed to show events and tell stories to people who, in past centuries, could not read.

ÉMILE GALLÉ (1846–1904) was a French artist who made colored glass vases and lampshades decorated with plants, insects, and other natural objects.

Stained-glass windows are made by fitting pieces of colored glass into lead channels and then joining the pieces of lead together by soldering (melting metal into the joints).

LOUIS COMFORT TIFFANY (1848–1933) was an American artist and designer famous for making stained-glass objects including windows, jewelry, and lamps.

RENÉ LALIQUE (1860–1945) was a French designer known for making beautiful glass vases, jewelry, and ornaments. He also made glass screens and columns for decorating buildings and ocean liners.

The Future of Glass

Designers are thinking up exciting new uses for glass. Imagine living in a home with light-sensitive windows that darken automatically in bright sunshine. If you had windows that you could darken at night, you wouldn't need curtains. Bright sunshine can be a problem for drivers. Car windows that darken automatically would ease this problem. Imagine a skyscraper with glass walls that are also giant video screens. The wonderful things we continue to learn to do with glass make us realize how much we wouldn't want to live without it!

NEW TYPES OF GLASS and glass coatings are being developed for electronic products. Screens for cell phones, tablets, and other devices made from this glass will be easier to use in bright light.

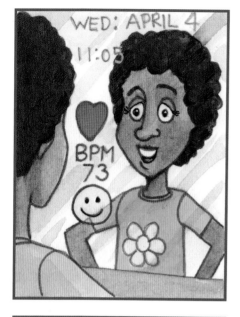

MIRROR MIRROR. Scientists are developing a special kind of mirror that can assess the health of anyone who stands in front of it.

Vitrification changes radioactive waste into blocks of glass, stopping it from escaping into the environment. Processes like these will help to keep our planet clean in the future.

IN THE FUTURE, glass may become an increasingly popular packaging material once again because it does not taint, contaminate, or react with its contents, and it is also totally recyclable.

SMART DESK. Using glass and technology, designers are developing exciting new ways to work and study. In the future, your desk might have a glass top that is also a touch-sensitive computer screen.

Glossary

Archeologist A scientist who studies human history, especially by digging up and examining the remains of people and their activities.

Astronomer A scientist who studies the stars, galaxies, planets, moons, and other bodies in the universe.

Atmosphere The gases that surround Earth and some other bodies.

Crystal Any solid material made of particles (atoms or molecules) arranged in a regular, repeating pattern.

Double glazing The process of creating a window from two sheets of glass with a small gap between them.

Flux A substance that lowers the melting point of sand, which helps make it easier to produce glass.

Former The main substance used in making or "forming" glass (usually silica, or sand).

Galaxy Millions or billions of stars traveling through space together, with giant clouds of gas and dust. We live in a galaxy called the Milky Way.

Germ A microscopic organism, especially one that causes disease.

Hide The skin of an animal.

Hubble Space Telescope An instrument in space that has been used by astronomers to study distant parts of the universe since 1990.

Insulation A material that stops or slows the spread of heat, sound, or electricity.

Laminated glass A type of safety glass that holds together even if the glass breaks.

Lava Liquid rock that erupts from volcanoes, and the same rock when cool and hard.

Lens A piece of glass or another transparent material shaped so that it forms an image by bending light rays.

Meteorite A piece of rock or natural metal that has fallen to Earth from space and survived its impact with the ground.

Middle Ages The name given to the period of European history between the fifth and fifteenth centuries.

Molten Made liquid by being heated to a very high temperature.

Organism A living plant or animal.

Primary mirror The main or biggest reflecting surface in an optical instrument such as a telescope.

Prism A piece of glass or other transparent material, often triangular in shape, used for separating white light into the colors of which it is made up.

Radioactive Giving out particles or rays by a process called radioactive decay.

Roman Empire A group of nations and tribes, mainly around the Mediterranean Sea, that were conquered and then governed by the Ancient Romans.

Secondary mirror The second, or smaller, reflecting surface inside an optical instrument such as a telescope. It reflects light from the larger primary mirror.

Stabilizer A substance that stops glass from dissolving or crumbling once it cools and hardens.

Tektite A small black piece of glass formed when a meteorite hits the ground and sends out splashes of molten rock. Each splash cools down to form a tektite.

Tempered glass A type of safety glass that forms small rounded crumbs of glass instead of sharp splinters when it breaks. Also called toughened glass.

Vitrification The process of changing a substance into glass by heating it to a very high temperature with glass-forming materials.

Index

Top Glassmakers

George Ravenscroft (1632–1683)
Ravenscroft learned about glassmaking while working in Venice. In 1666 he returned to England and started his own glassmaking business. The glass being made in England at that time would become cloudy and cracked after a year or two, a problem called crizzling. Ravenscroft experimented with different materials. He discovered that adding lead oxide improved the glass. What became known as lead glass was a sparkling, hard glass that lasted longer and didn't suffer from crizzling.

Joseph Paxton (1803–1865)
Paxton was an English gardener who worked for the Duke of Devonshire. He built an iron and glass conservatory at the duke's stately home, Chatsworth. When he heard that all the designs for a building to house the Great Exhibition in London had been rejected, he sent his own design based on his conservatory. It was accepted, because it was inexpensive and quick and easy to build. The building became famous as the Crystal Palace. Paxton received a knighthood for his work, which marked the beginning of glass as a building material.

Sir Alastair Pilkington (1920–1995)
After studying mechanical engineering at Cambridge University in England, Pilkington went to work for the Pilkington glass company. (He had no connection with the Pilkington family who founded the company, it was just a funny coincidence.) While working there he came up with the idea of making flat glass by floating it on molten tin. He perfected the method in 1959, making it possible to produce high-quality flat glass without having to grind and polish it.

Prince Rupert's Drop

When a blob of molten glass is dropped into cold water, it quickly cools and sets hard, forming a glass droplet with a long, thin tail. It looks a little like a glass tadpole. A piece of glass like this is called a Prince Rupert's Drop, and it behaves in a very strange way.

The head of a Prince Rupert's Drop is surprisingly strong. In fact, you can hit it with a hammer and it won't break. However, the tail of a Prince Rupert's Drop is very different from the head. If the thin tail is broken, the whole thing explodes! This is because the glass on the outside of a Prince Rupert's Drop cools faster than the glass inside. This produces enormous forces that make the glass explode dramatically when it breaks.